JR. GRAPHIC MONSTER STORIES

GREMLINS!

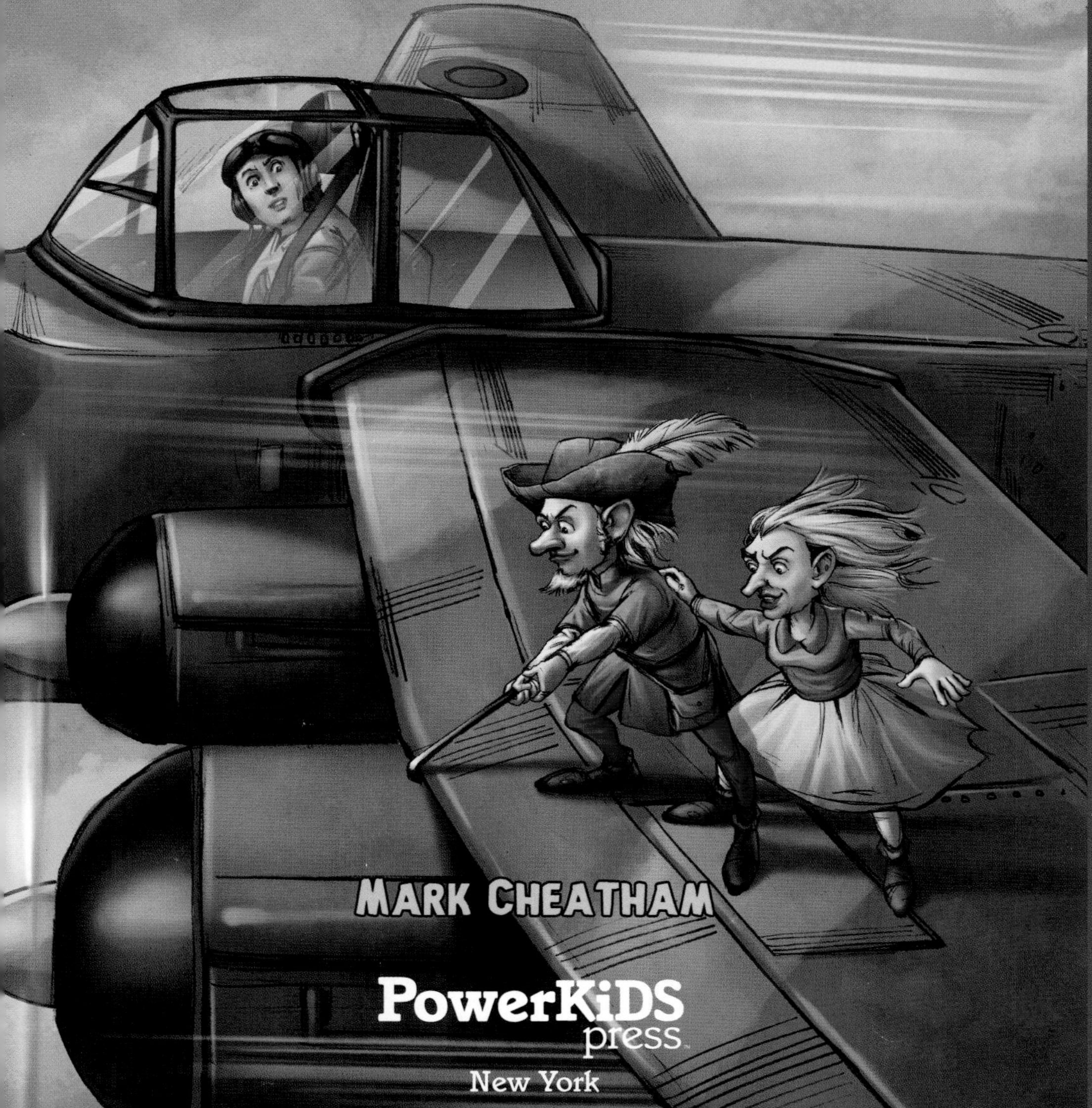

MARK CHEATHAM

PowerKiDS press
New York

Published in 2014 by The Rosen Publishing Group, Inc.
29 East 21st Street, New York, NY 10010

First Edition

Editor: Joanne Randolph
Book Design: Planman Technologies
Illustrations: Planman Technologies

Library of Congress Cataloging-in-Publication Data

Cheatham, Mark.
 Gremlins! / by Mark Cheatham.
     pages cm. — (Jr. graphic monster stories)
 Includes index.
 ISBN 978-1-4777-6215-8 (library) — ISBN 978-1-4777-6216-5 (pbk.) —
 ISBN 978-1-4777-6217-2 (6-pack)
 1. Monsters. I. Title.
 GR825.C44 2014
 001.944—dc23

                                  2013026280

Manufactured in the United States of America
CPSIA Compliance Information: Batch # W14PK1: For Further Information contact Rosen
Publishing, New York, New York at 1-800-237-9932

Contents

Main Characters

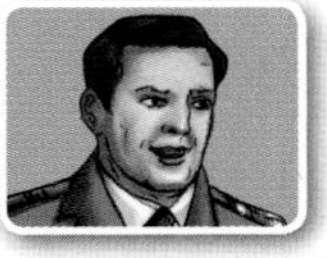

Hubert Griffith A British pilot with the Royal Air Force during World War II. In 1942, Griffith wrote a widely read article on the strange sightings of gremlins during combat missions.

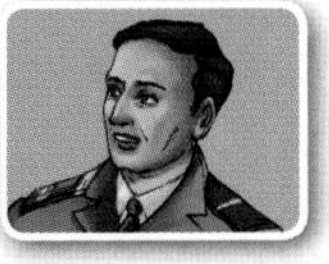

Mickey Rook A British pilot and friend of Hubert Griffith who widened Griffith's gremlin knowledge and helped end the threat from the gremlins.

Where Gremlins Come From

- It is thought that the ancient relatives of the gremlins may be the **leprechauns**. Tales of leprechauns come from ancient Irish legends. A leprechaun was often described as a bearded man about the height of a small child wearing a red or green jacket.
- Leprechauns loved to dance. Because of this, the leprechaun's main job was repairing shoes.
- The leprechaun kept his gold in a pot at the end of a rainbow. If a person captured a leprechaun, the leprechaun would grant him three wishes in exchange for his release.

Gremlins!

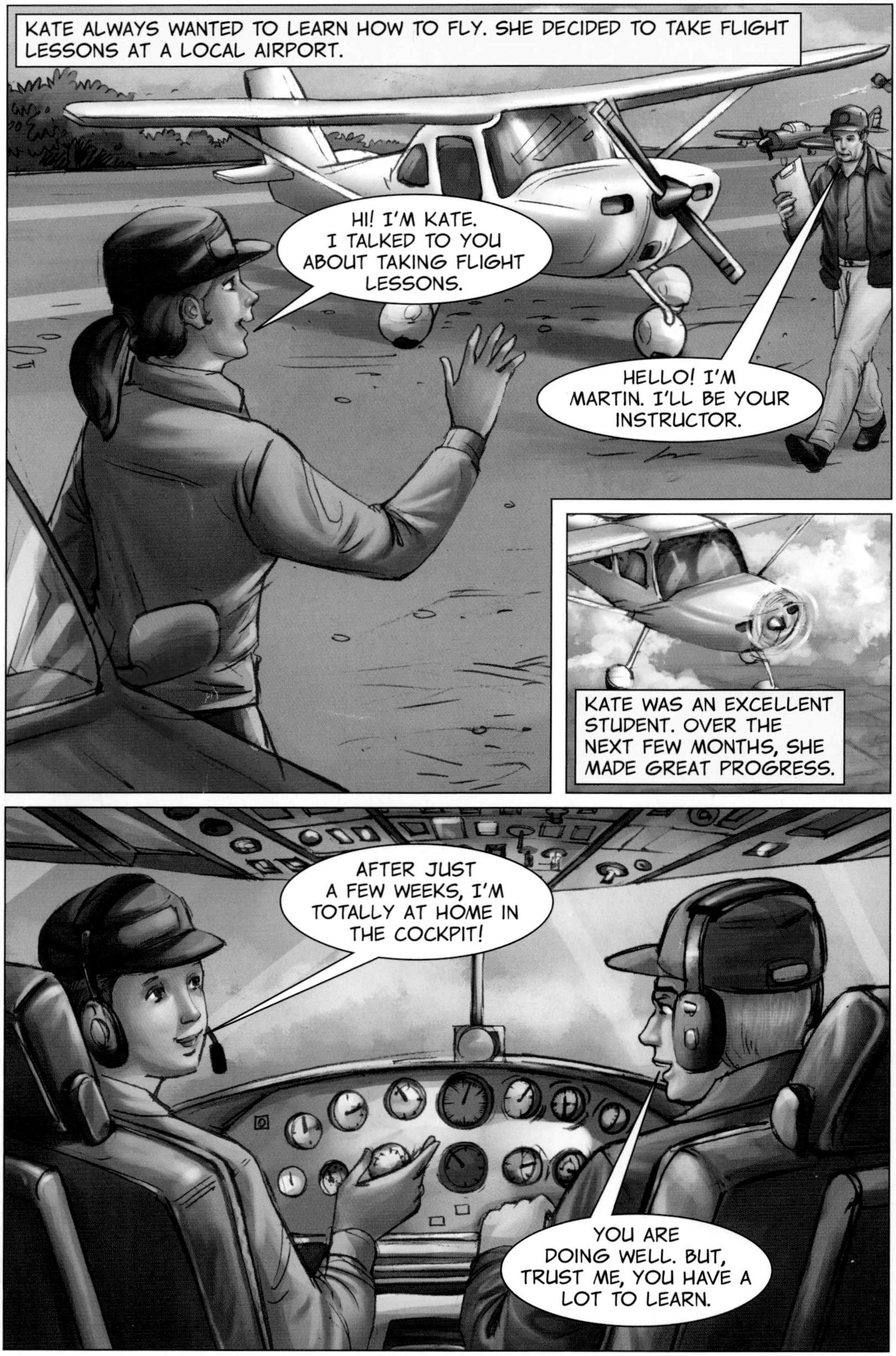
KATE ALWAYS WANTED TO LEARN HOW TO FLY. SHE DECIDED TO TAKE FLIGHT LESSONS AT A LOCAL AIRPORT.
HI! I'M KATE. I TALKED TO YOU ABOUT TAKING FLIGHT LESSONS.
HELLO! I'M MARTIN. I'LL BE YOUR INSTRUCTOR.
KATE WAS AN EXCELLENT STUDENT. OVER THE NEXT FEW MONTHS, SHE MADE GREAT PROGRESS.
AFTER JUST A FEW WEEKS, I'M TOTALLY AT HOME IN THE COCKPIT!
YOU ARE DOING WELL. BUT, TRUST ME, YOU HAVE A LOT TO LEARN.

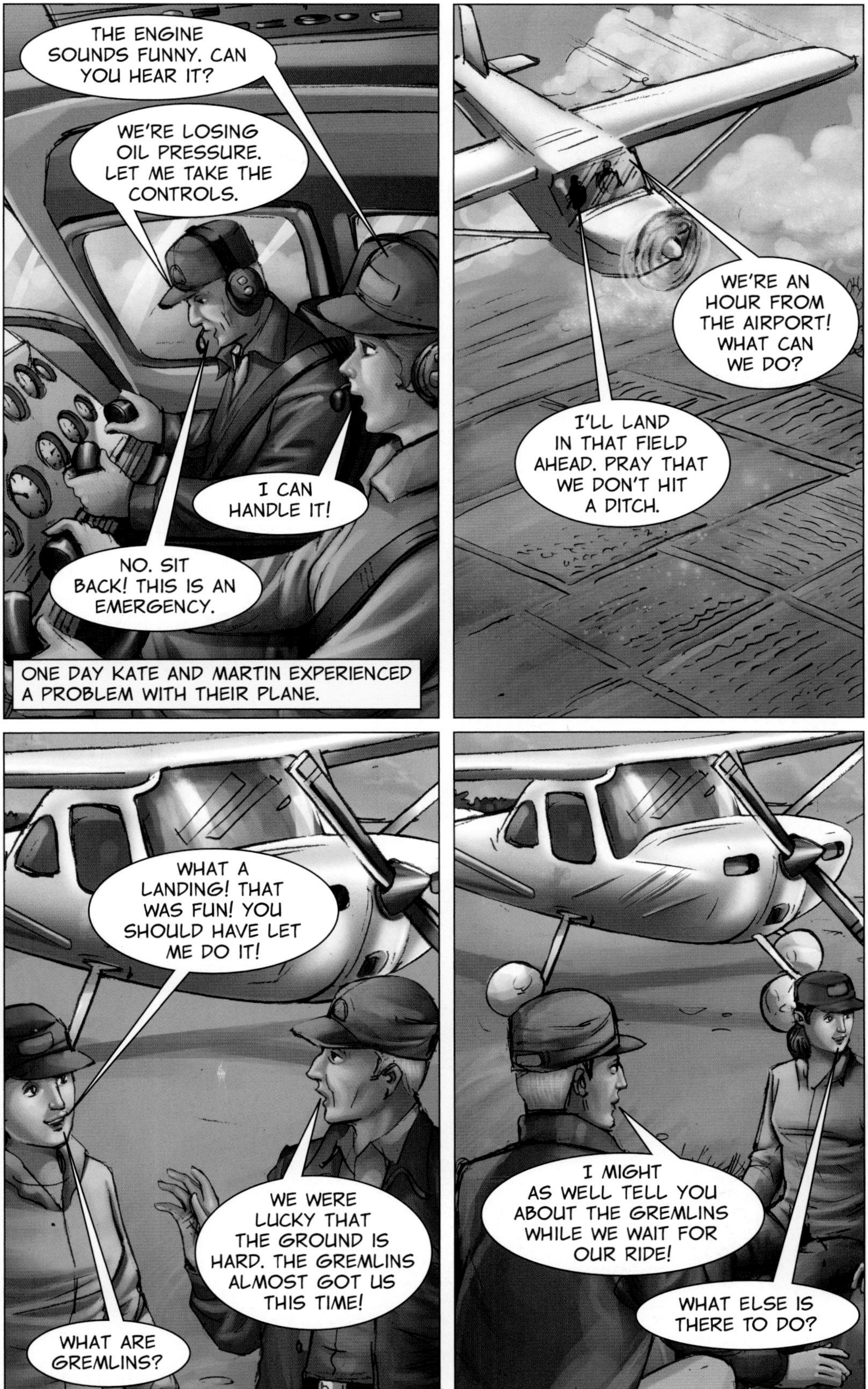
THE ENGINE SOUNDS FUNNY. CAN YOU HEAR IT?
WE'RE LOSING OIL PRESSURE. LET ME TAKE THE CONTROLS.
I CAN HANDLE IT!
NO. SIT BACK! THIS IS AN EMERGENCY.
ONE DAY KATE AND MARTIN EXPERIENCED A PROBLEM WITH THEIR PLANE.
WE'RE AN HOUR FROM THE AIRPORT! WHAT CAN WE DO?
I'LL LAND IN THAT FIELD AHEAD. PRAY THAT WE DON'T HIT A DITCH.
WHAT A LANDING! THAT WAS FUN! YOU SHOULD HAVE LET ME DO IT!
WE WERE LUCKY THAT THE GROUND IS HARD. THE GREMLINS ALMOST GOT US THIS TIME!
WHAT ARE GREMLINS?
I MIGHT AS WELL TELL YOU ABOUT THE GREMLINS WHILE WE WAIT FOR OUR RIDE!
WHAT ELSE IS THERE TO DO?

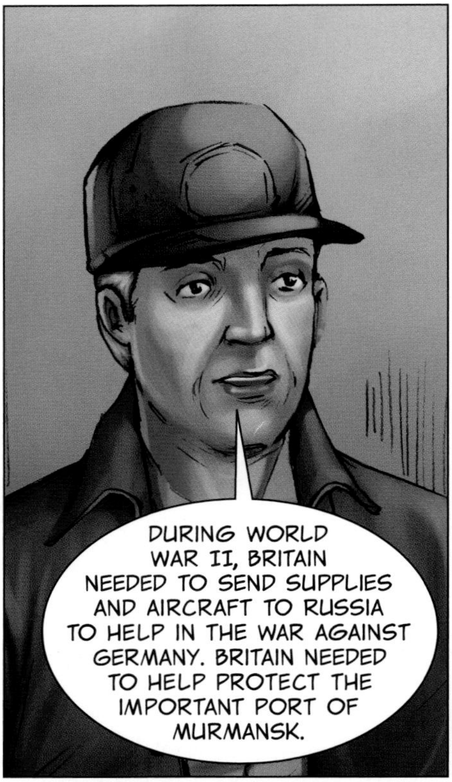
DURING WORLD WAR II, BRITAIN NEEDED TO SEND SUPPLIES AND AIRCRAFT TO RUSSIA TO HELP IN THE WAR AGAINST GERMANY. BRITAIN NEEDED TO HELP PROTECT THE IMPORTANT PORT OF MURMANSK.

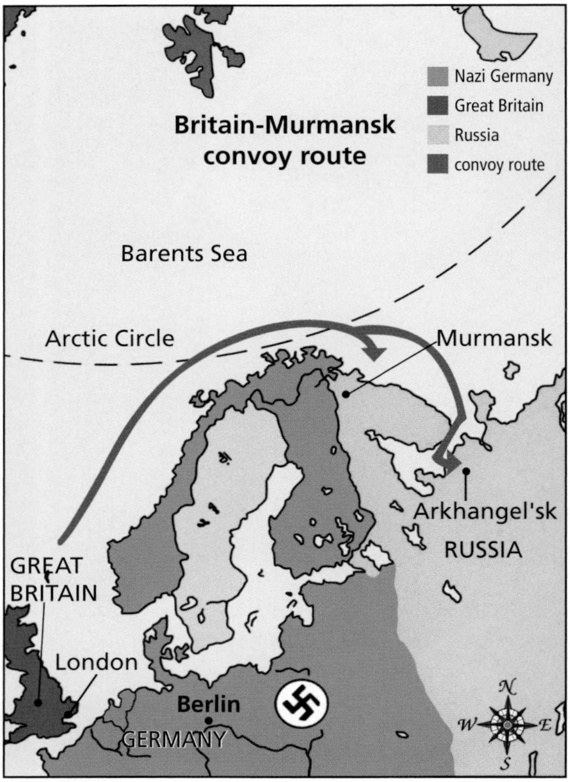
Britain-Murmansk convoy route
Nazi Germany
Great Britain
Russia
convoy route
Barents Sea
Arctic Circle
Murmansk
Arkhangel'sk
RUSSIA
GREAT BRITAIN
London
Berlin
GERMANY
N
W
E
S

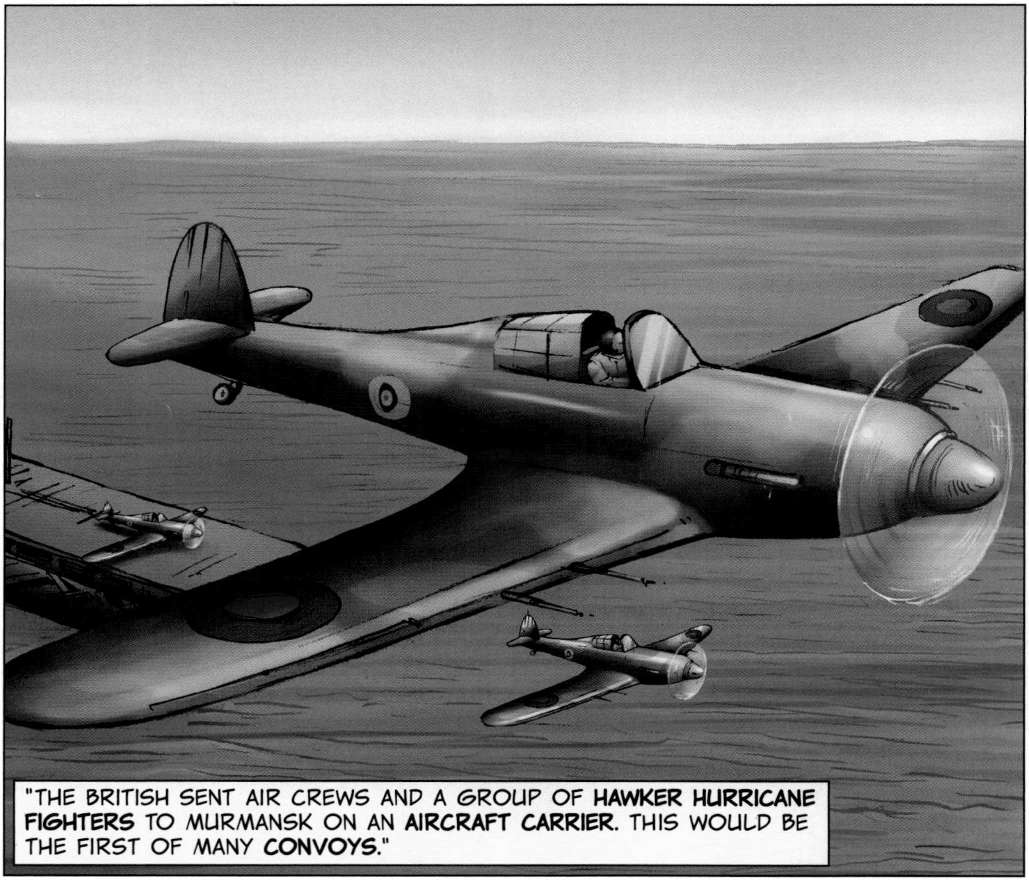
"THE BRITISH SENT AIR CREWS AND A GROUP OF **HAWKER HURRICANE FIGHTERS** TO MURMANSK ON AN **AIRCRAFT CARRIER**. THIS WOULD BE THE FIRST OF MANY **CONVOYS**."

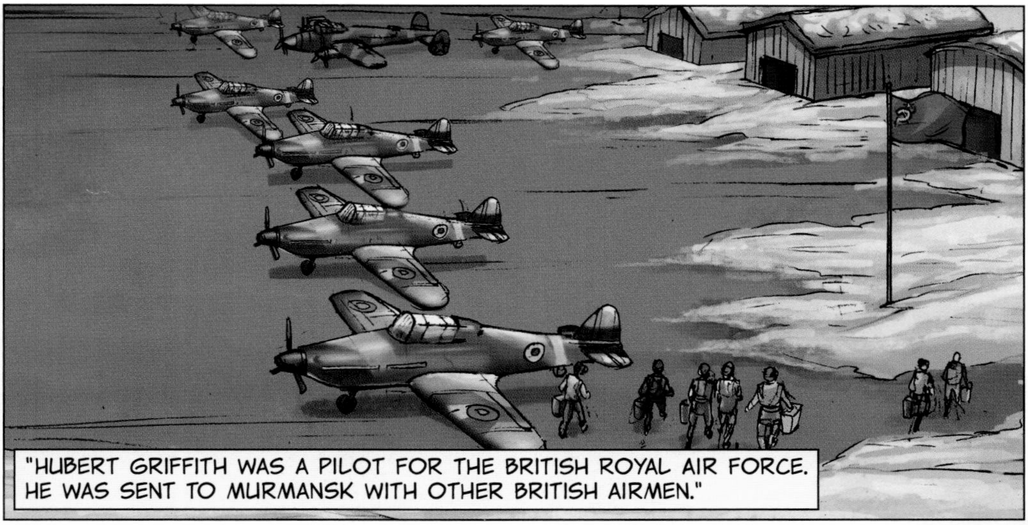
"HUBERT GRIFFITH WAS A PILOT FOR THE BRITISH ROYAL AIR FORCE. HE WAS SENT TO MURMANSK WITH OTHER BRITISH AIRMEN."

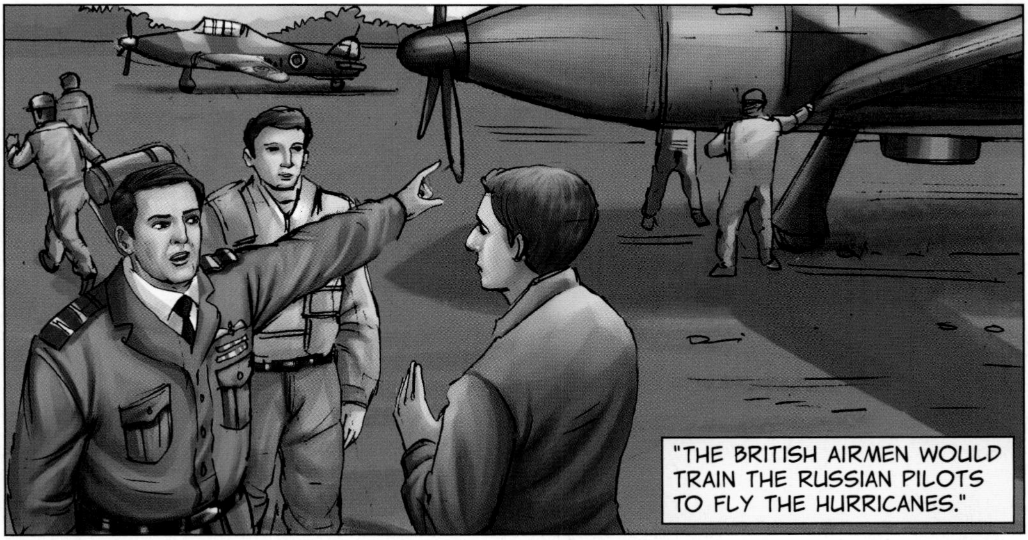
"THE BRITISH AIRMEN WOULD TRAIN THE RUSSIAN PILOTS TO FLY THE HURRICANES."

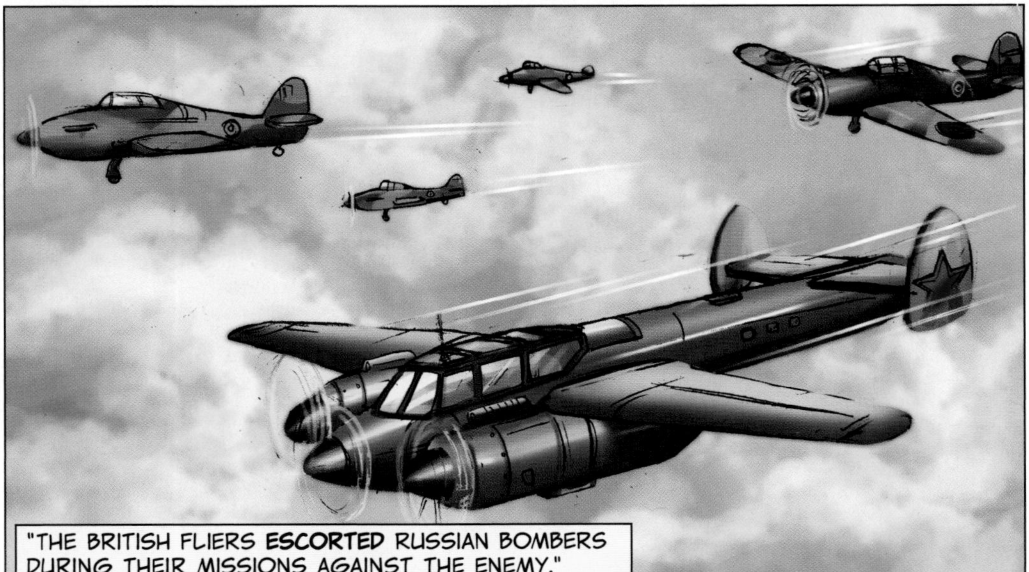
"THE BRITISH FLIERS **ESCORTED** RUSSIAN BOMBERS DURING THEIR MISSIONS AGAINST THE ENEMY."

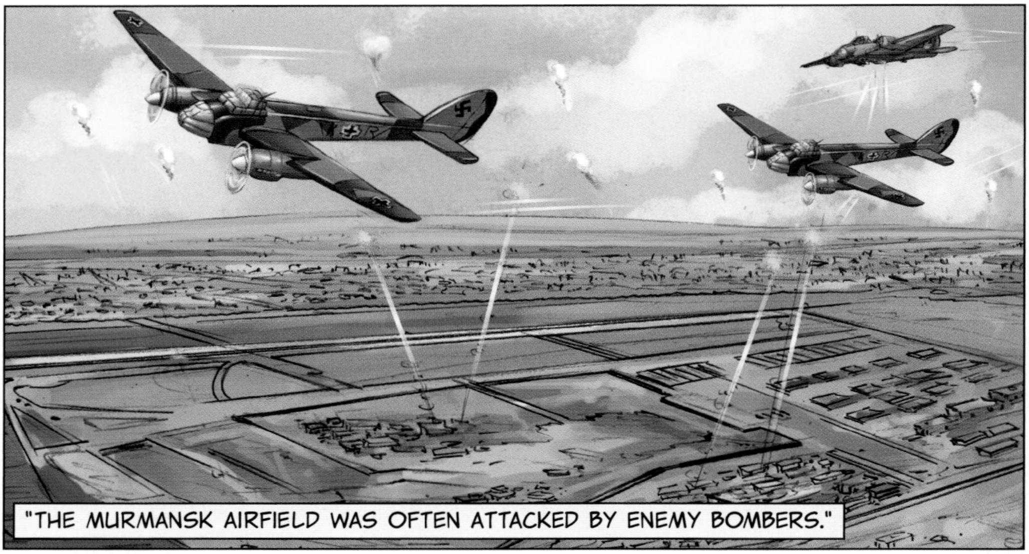
"THE MURMANSK AIRFIELD WAS OFTEN ATTACKED BY ENEMY BOMBERS."

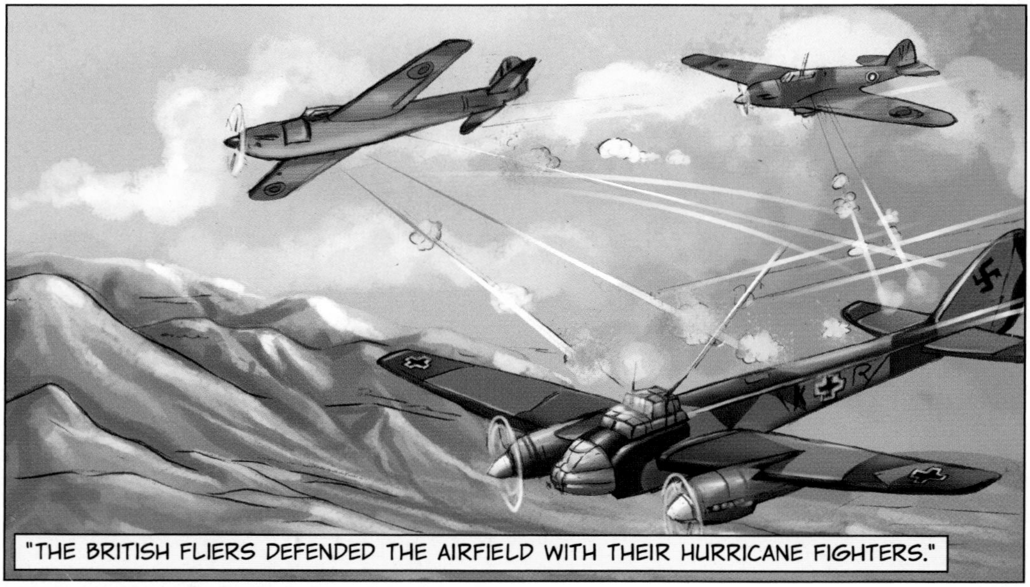
"THE BRITISH FLIERS DEFENDED THE AIRFIELD WITH THEIR HURRICANE FIGHTERS."

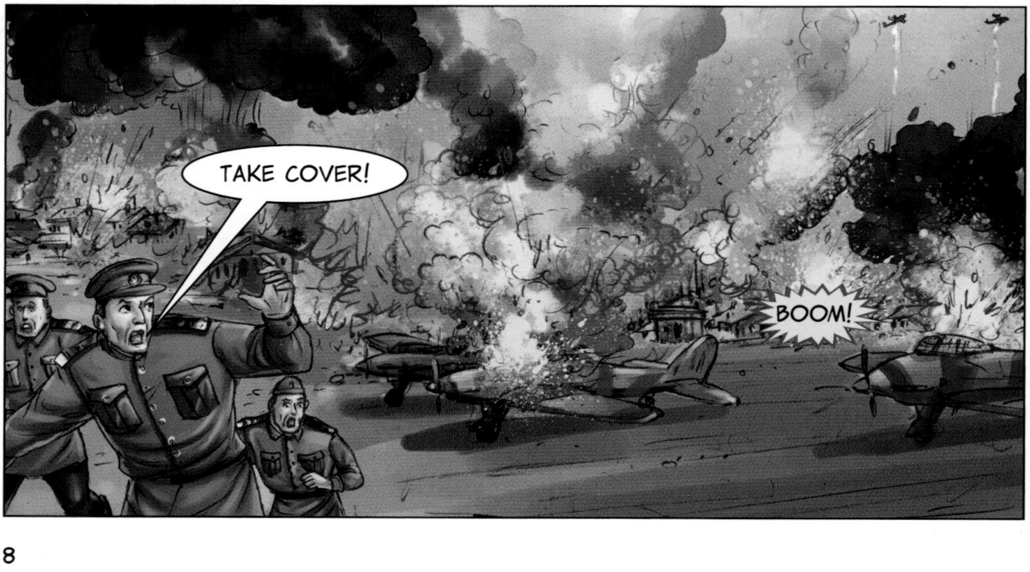
TAKE COVER!
BOOM!

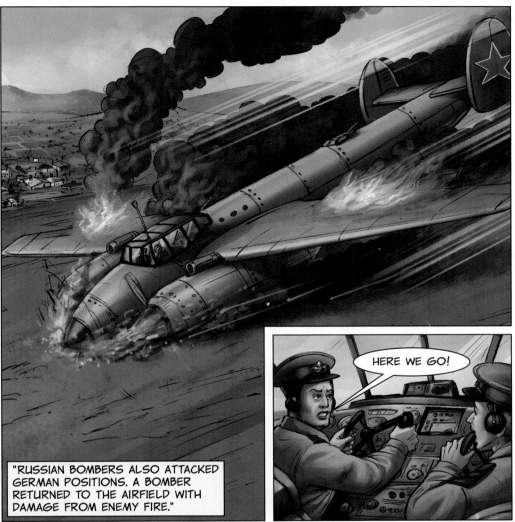

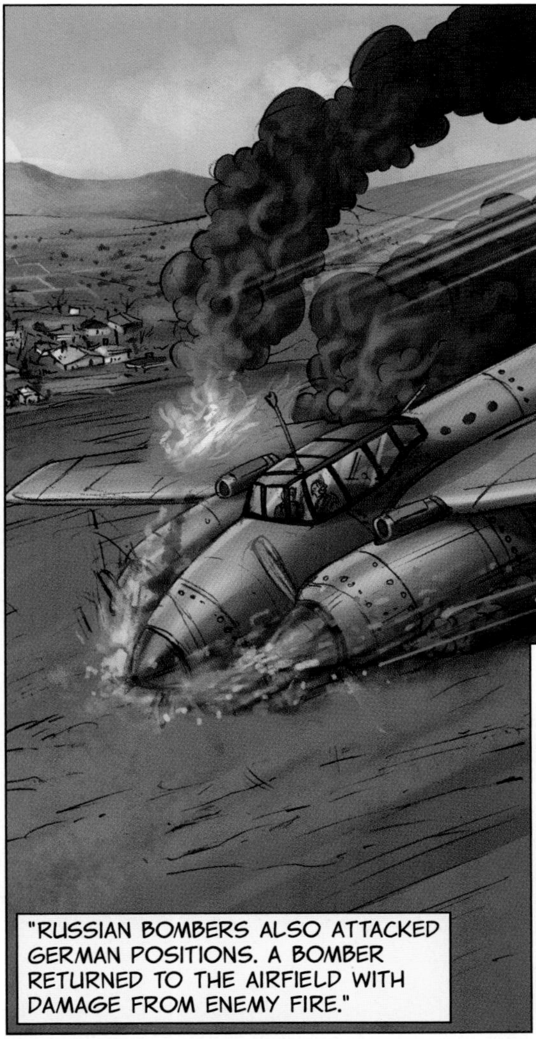
"RUSSIAN BOMBERS ALSO ATTACKED GERMAN POSITIONS. A BOMBER RETURNED TO THE AIRFIELD WITH DAMAGE FROM ENEMY FIRE."

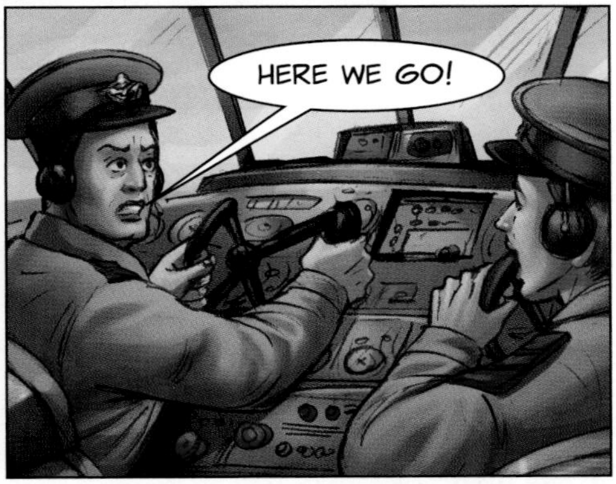
HERE WE GO!

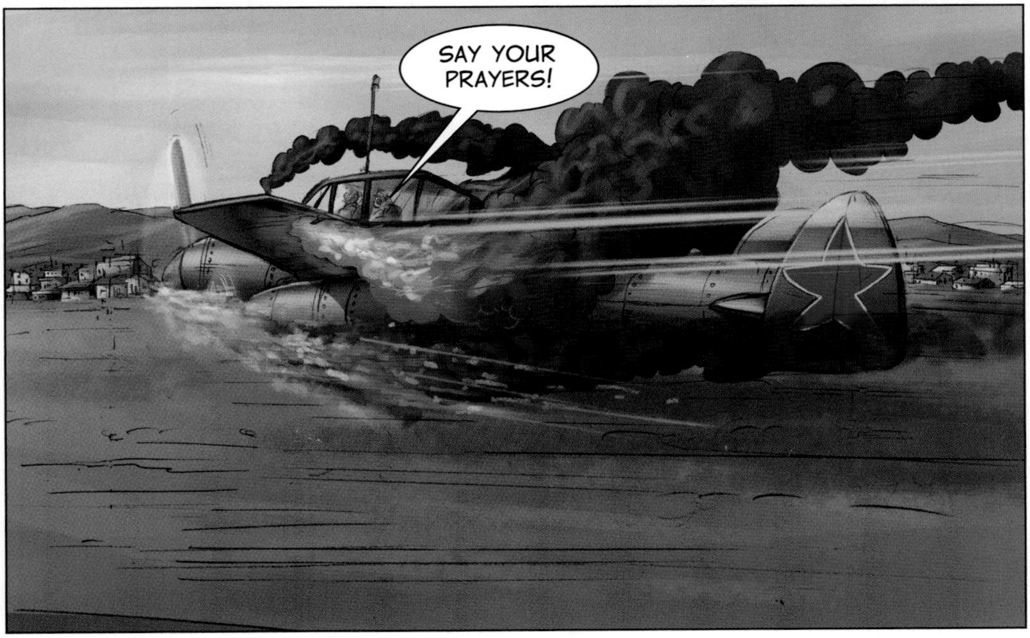
SAY YOUR PRAYERS!

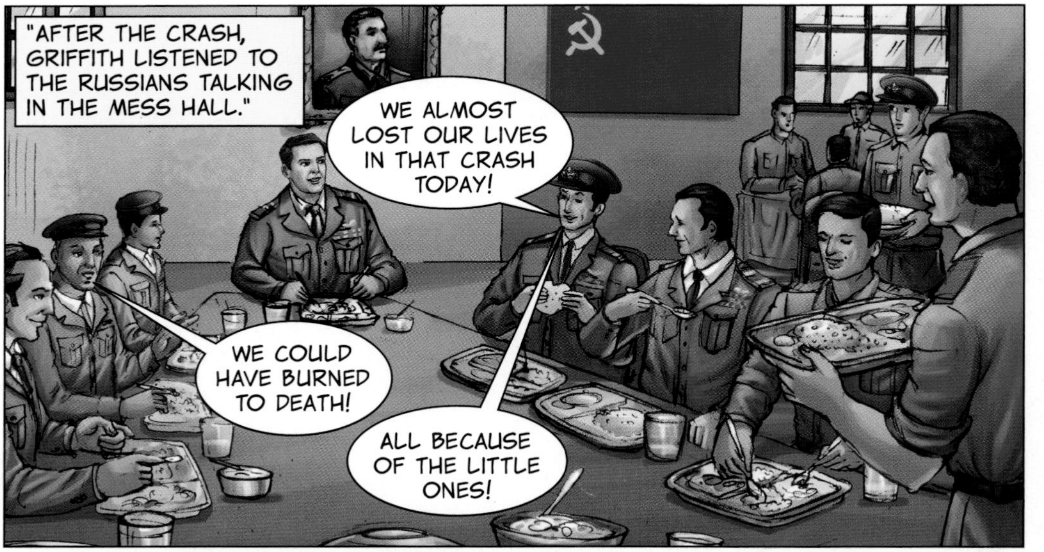
"AFTER THE CRASH, GRIFFITH LISTENED TO THE RUSSIANS TALKING IN THE MESS HALL."
WE ALMOST LOST OUR LIVES IN THAT CRASH TODAY!
WE COULD HAVE BURNED TO DEATH!
ALL BECAUSE OF THE LITTLE ONES!

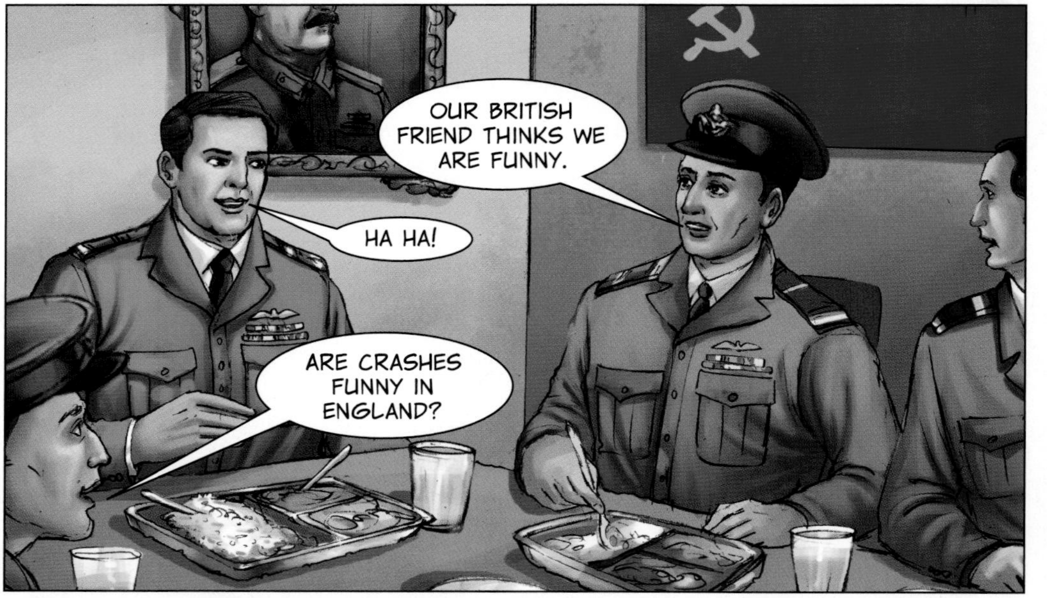
OUR BRITISH FRIEND THINKS WE ARE FUNNY.
HA HA!
ARE CRASHES FUNNY IN ENGLAND?

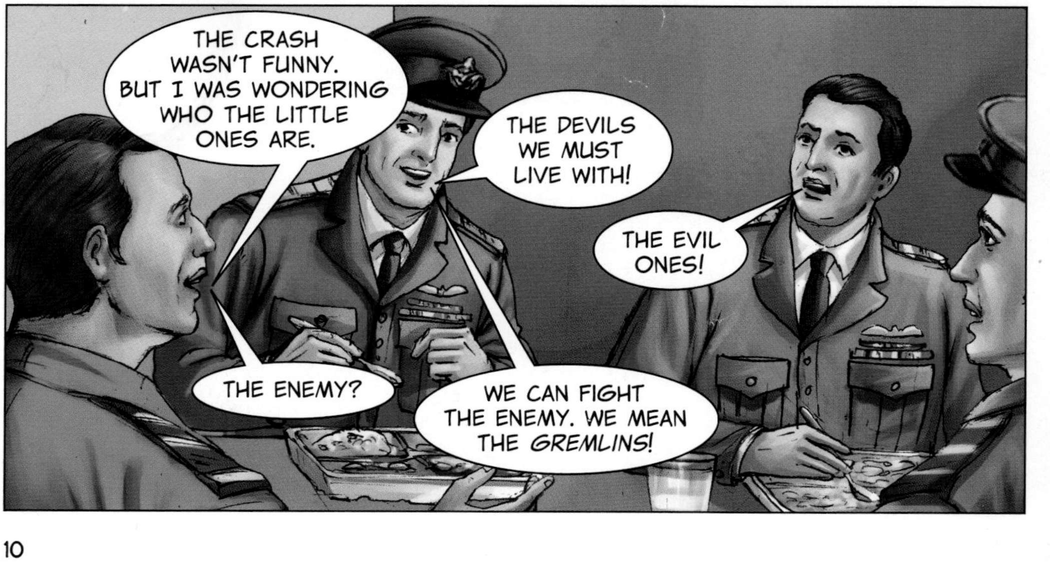
THE CRASH WASN'T FUNNY. BUT I WAS WONDERING WHO THE LITTLE ONES ARE.
THE DEVILS WE MUST LIVE WITH!
THE EVIL ONES!
THE ENEMY?
WE CAN FIGHT THE ENEMY. WE MEAN THE *GREMLINS*!

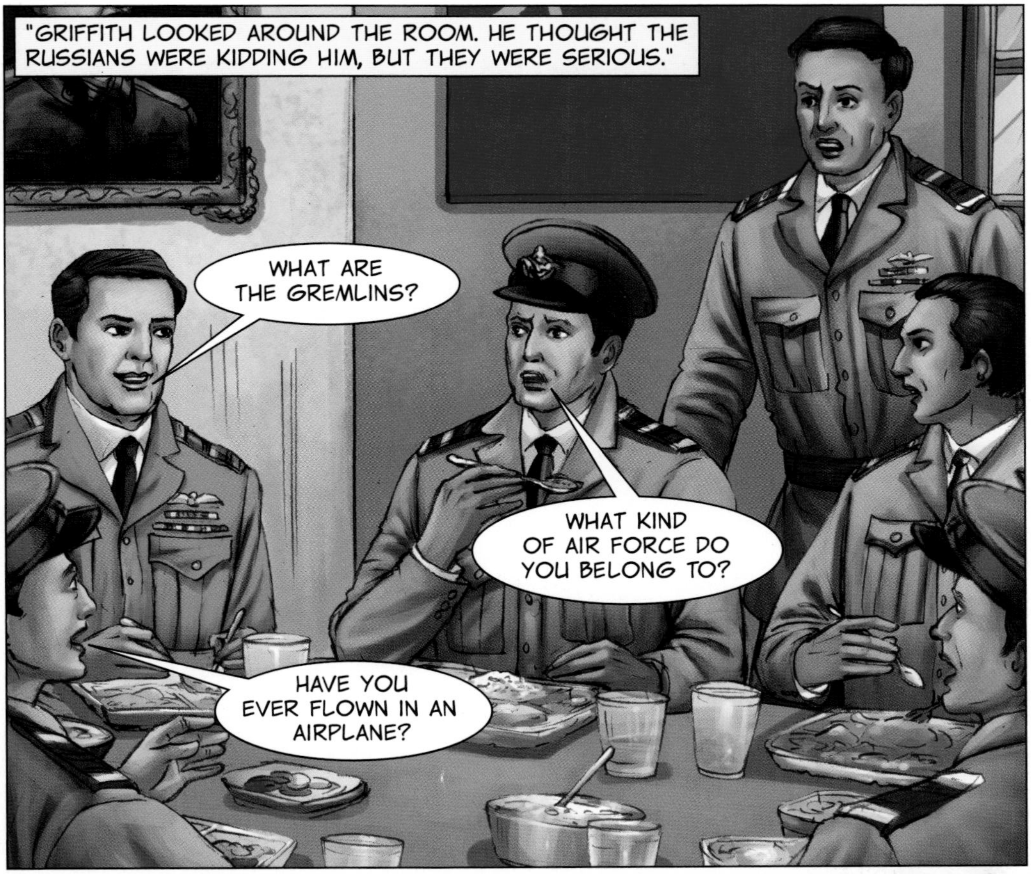
"GRIFFITH LOOKED AROUND THE ROOM. HE THOUGHT THE RUSSIANS WERE KIDDING HIM, BUT THEY WERE SERIOUS."
WHAT ARE THE GREMLINS?
WHAT KIND OF AIR FORCE DO YOU BELONG TO?
HAVE YOU EVER FLOWN IN AN AIRPLANE?

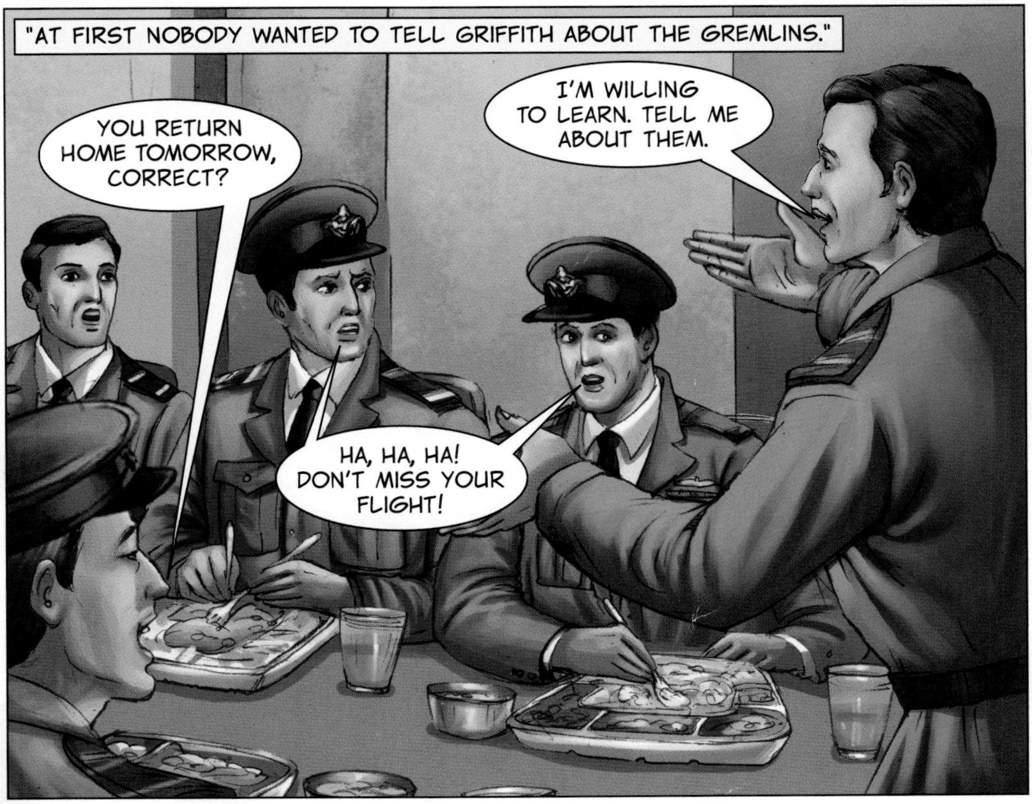
"AT FIRST NOBODY WANTED TO TELL GRIFFITH ABOUT THE GREMLINS."
YOU RETURN HOME TOMORROW, CORRECT?
I'M WILLING TO LEARN. TELL ME ABOUT THEM.
HA, HA, HA! DON'T MISS YOUR FLIGHT!

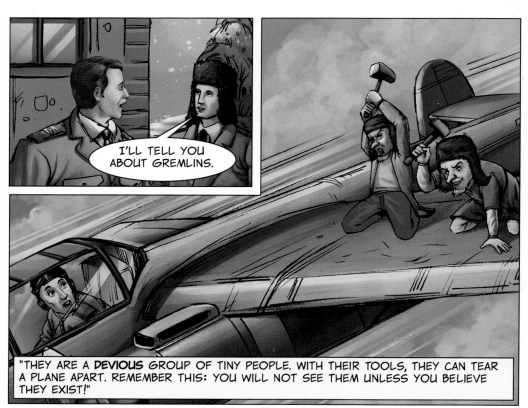

I'LL TELL YOU ABOUT GREMLINS.

"THEY ARE A **DEVIOUS** GROUP OF TINY PEOPLE. WITH THEIR TOOLS, THEY CAN TEAR A PLANE APART. REMEMBER THIS: YOU WILL NOT SEE THEM UNLESS YOU BELIEVE THEY EXIST!"

"WHEN HIS MISSION IN RUSSIA WAS OVER, GRIFFITH RETURNED HOME TO BRITAIN THINKING ABOUT WHAT HE HAD LEARNED."

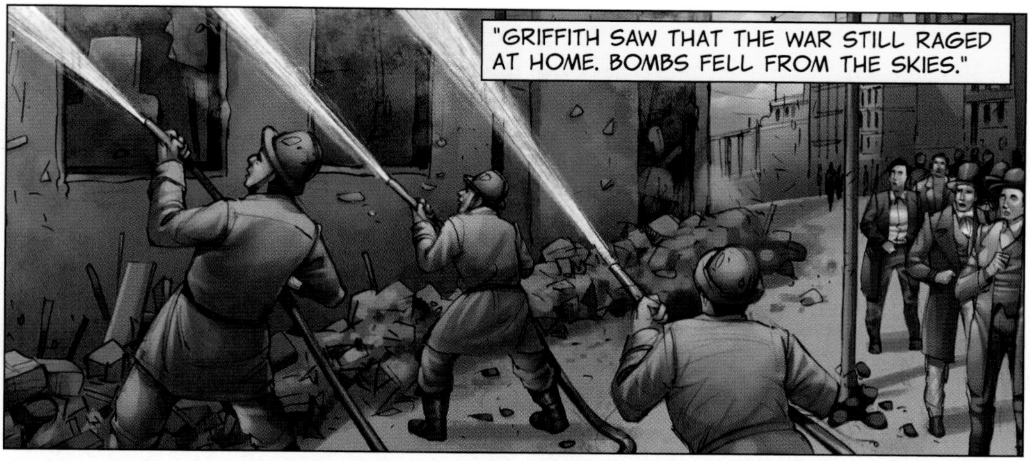
"GRIFFITH SAW THAT THE WAR STILL RAGED AT HOME. BOMBS FELL FROM THE SKIES."

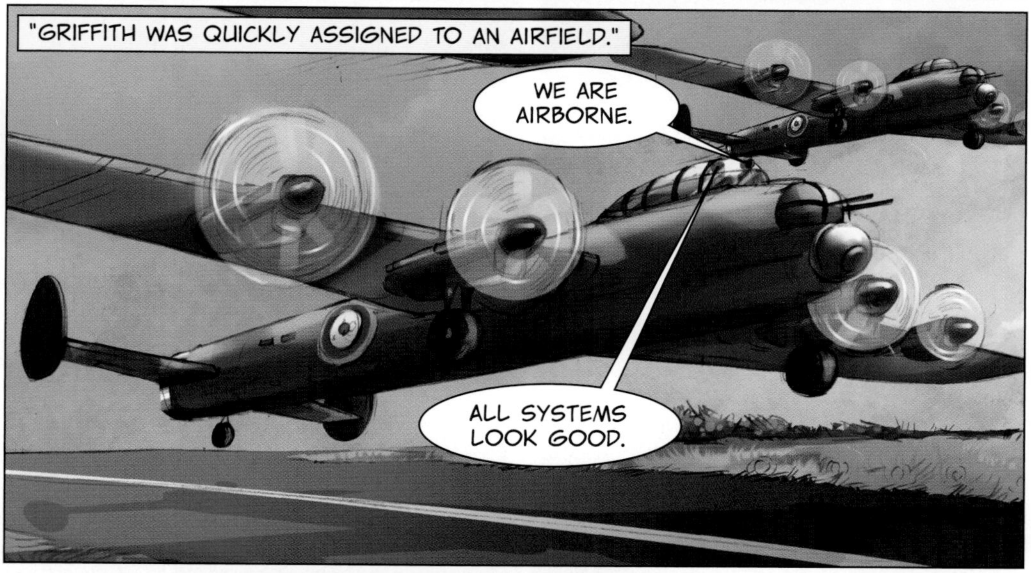
"GRIFFITH WAS QUICKLY ASSIGNED TO AN AIRFIELD."
WE ARE AIRBORNE.
ALL SYSTEMS LOOK GOOD.

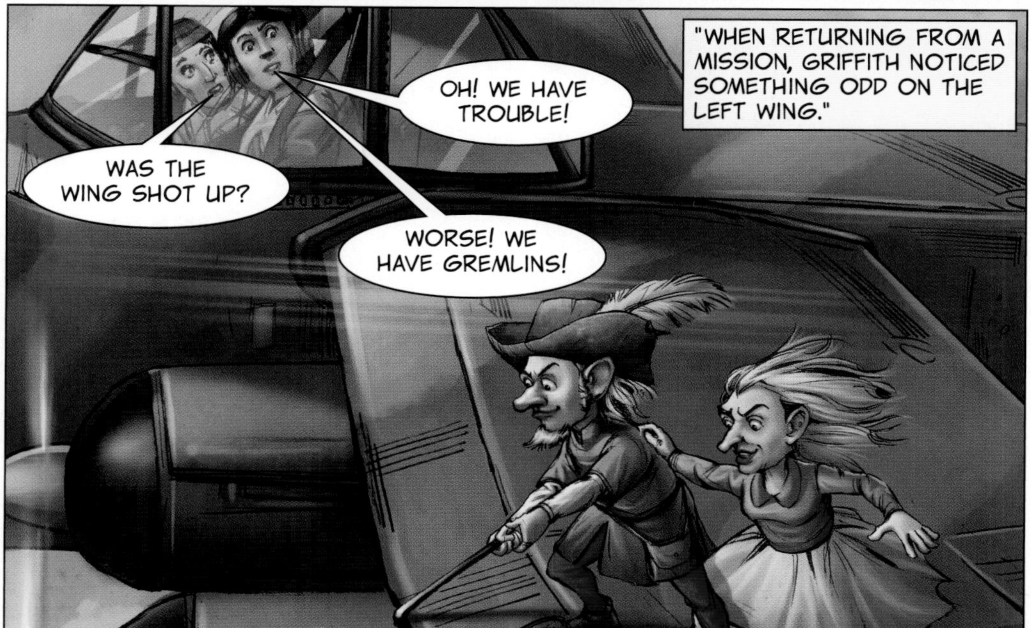
"WHEN RETURNING FROM A MISSION, GRIFFITH NOTICED SOMETHING ODD ON THE LEFT WING."
OH! WE HAVE TROUBLE!
WAS THE WING SHOT UP?
WORSE! WE HAVE GREMLINS!

"THE DAMAGE THE GREMLINS DID TO THE WING MADE THE PLANE HARD FOR GRIFFITH TO CONTROL."

HOLD ON!

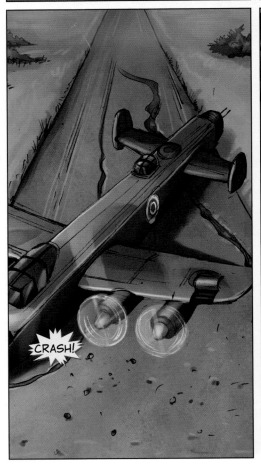

CRASH!

THERE THEY ARE AGAIN!

WHO? HUBERT, DID YOU HIT YOUR HEAD? ARE YOU OKAY?

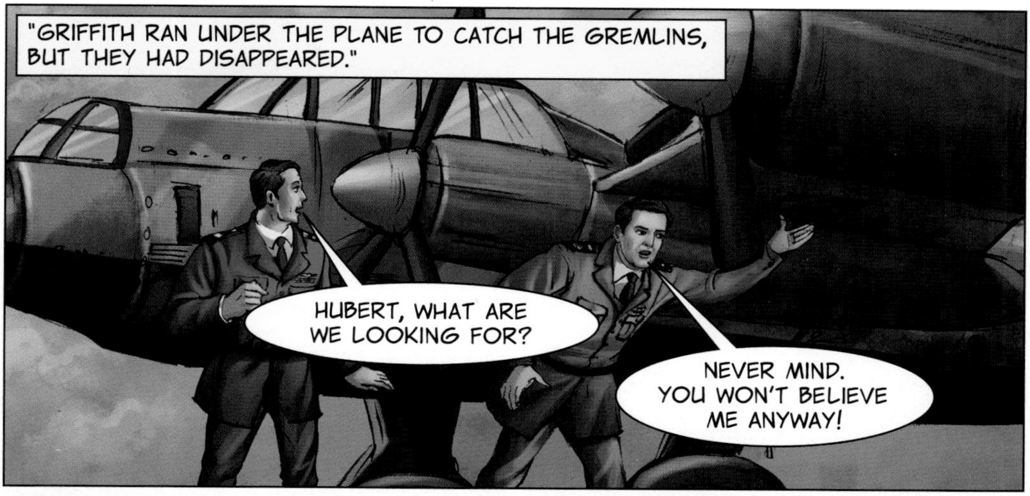
"GRIFFITH RAN UNDER THE PLANE TO CATCH THE GREMLINS, BUT THEY HAD DISAPPEARED."
HUBERT, WHAT ARE WE LOOKING FOR?
NEVER MIND. YOU WON'T BELIEVE ME ANYWAY!

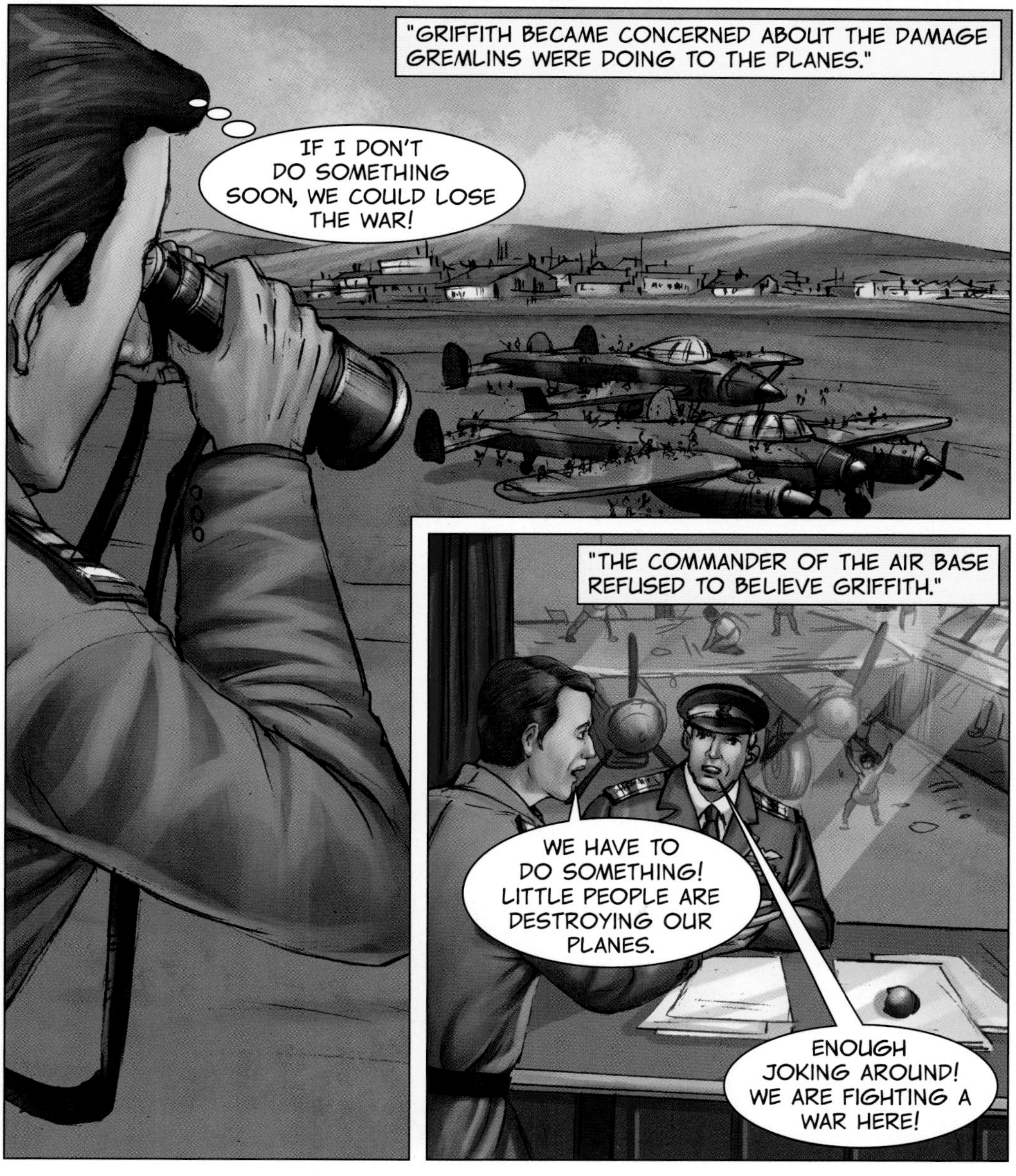
"GRIFFITH BECAME CONCERNED ABOUT THE DAMAGE GREMLINS WERE DOING TO THE PLANES."
IF I DON'T DO SOMETHING SOON, WE COULD LOSE THE WAR!
"THE COMMANDER OF THE AIR BASE REFUSED TO BELIEVE GRIFFITH."
WE HAVE TO DO SOMETHING! LITTLE PEOPLE ARE DESTROYING OUR PLANES.
ENOUGH JOKING AROUND! WE ARE FIGHTING A WAR HERE!

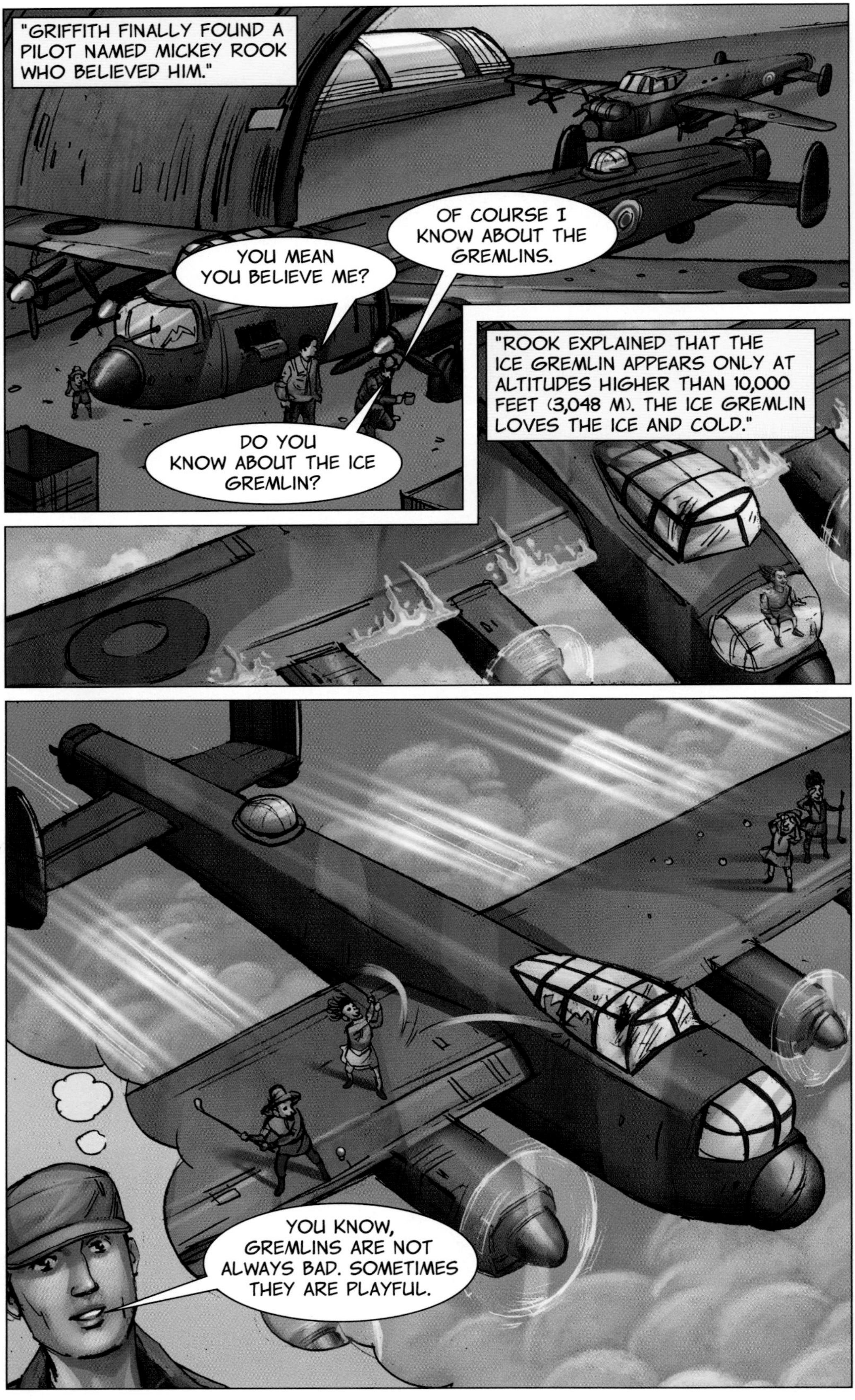
"GRIFFITH FINALLY FOUND A PILOT NAMED MICKEY ROOK WHO BELIEVED HIM."
YOU MEAN YOU BELIEVE ME?
OF COURSE I KNOW ABOUT THE GREMLINS.
DO YOU KNOW ABOUT THE ICE GREMLIN?
"ROOK EXPLAINED THAT THE ICE GREMLIN APPEARS ONLY AT ALTITUDES HIGHER THAN 10,000 FEET (3,048 M). THE ICE GREMLIN LOVES THE ICE AND COLD."
YOU KNOW, GREMLINS ARE NOT ALWAYS BAD. SOMETIMES THEY ARE PLAYFUL.

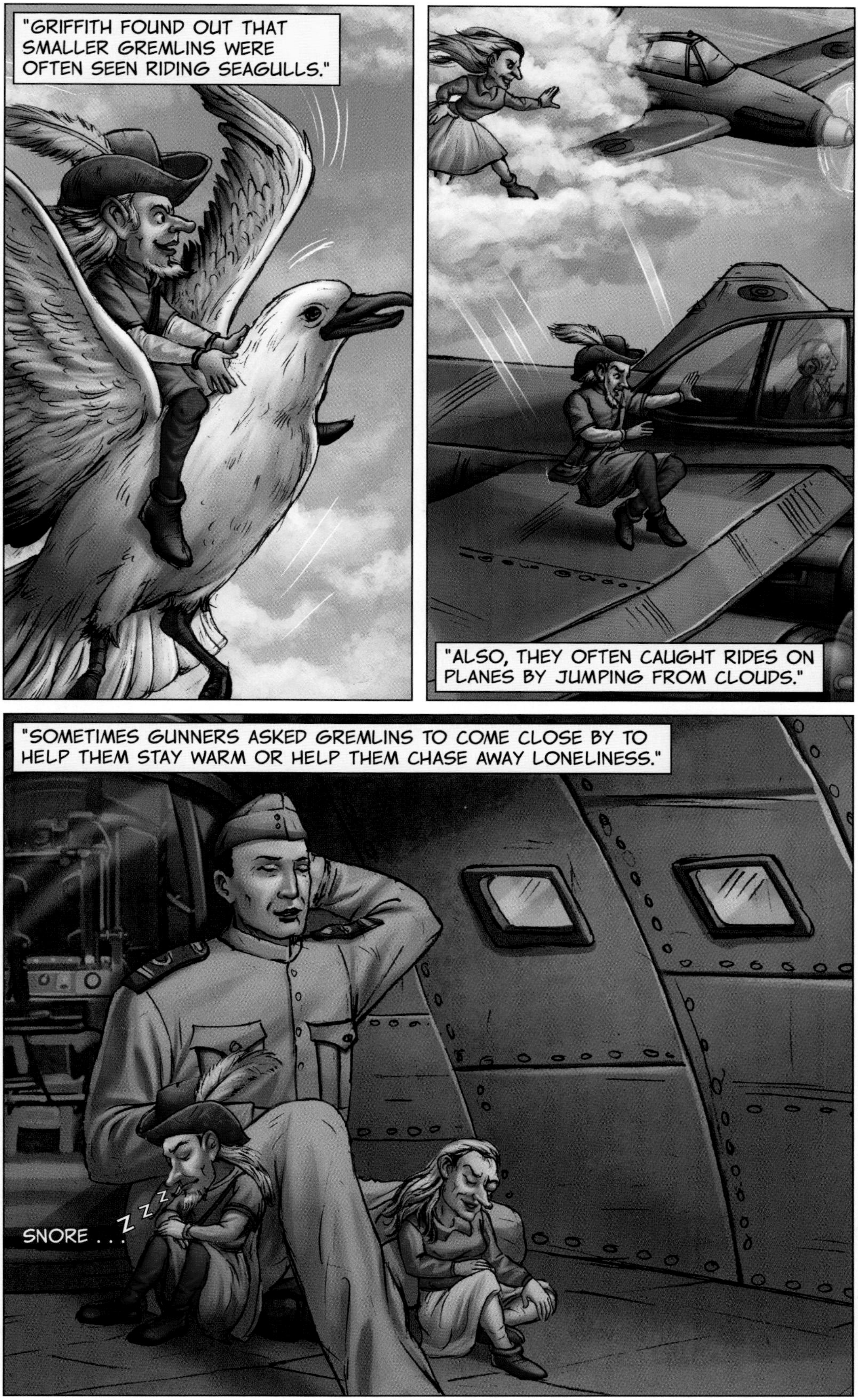
"GRIFFITH FOUND OUT THAT SMALLER GREMLINS WERE OFTEN SEEN RIDING SEAGULLS."
"ALSO, THEY OFTEN CAUGHT RIDES ON PLANES BY JUMPING FROM CLOUDS."
"SOMETIMES GUNNERS ASKED GREMLINS TO COME CLOSE BY TO HELP THEM STAY WARM OR HELP THEM CHASE AWAY LONELINESS."
SNORE . . . Z Z Z

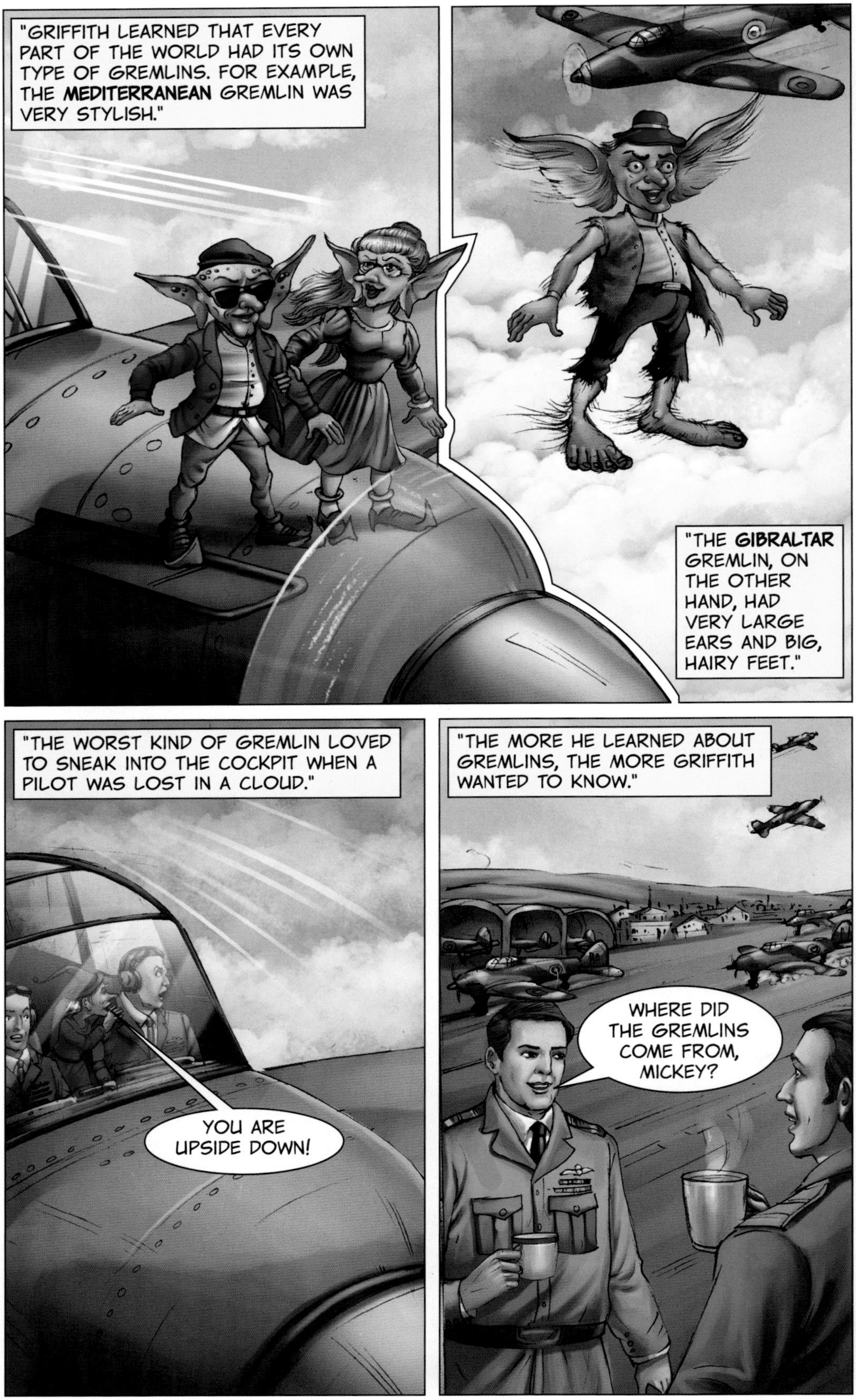
"GRIFFITH LEARNED THAT EVERY PART OF THE WORLD HAD ITS OWN TYPE OF GREMLINS. FOR EXAMPLE, THE **MEDITERRANEAN** GREMLIN WAS VERY STYLISH."
"THE **GIBRALTAR** GREMLIN, ON THE OTHER HAND, HAD VERY LARGE EARS AND BIG, HAIRY FEET."
"THE WORST KIND OF GREMLIN LOVED TO SNEAK INTO THE COCKPIT WHEN A PILOT WAS LOST IN A CLOUD."
YOU ARE UPSIDE DOWN!
"THE MORE HE LEARNED ABOUT GREMLINS, THE MORE GRIFFITH WANTED TO KNOW."
WHERE DID THE GREMLINS COME FROM, MICKEY?

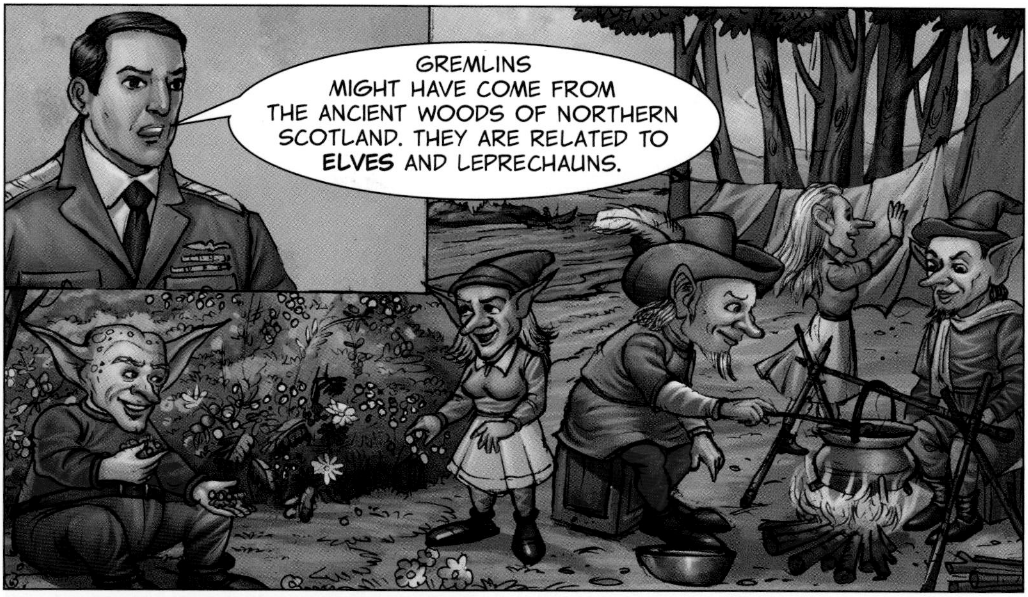
GREMLINS MIGHT HAVE COME FROM THE ANCIENT WOODS OF NORTHERN SCOTLAND. THEY ARE RELATED TO **ELVES** AND LEPRECHAUNS.

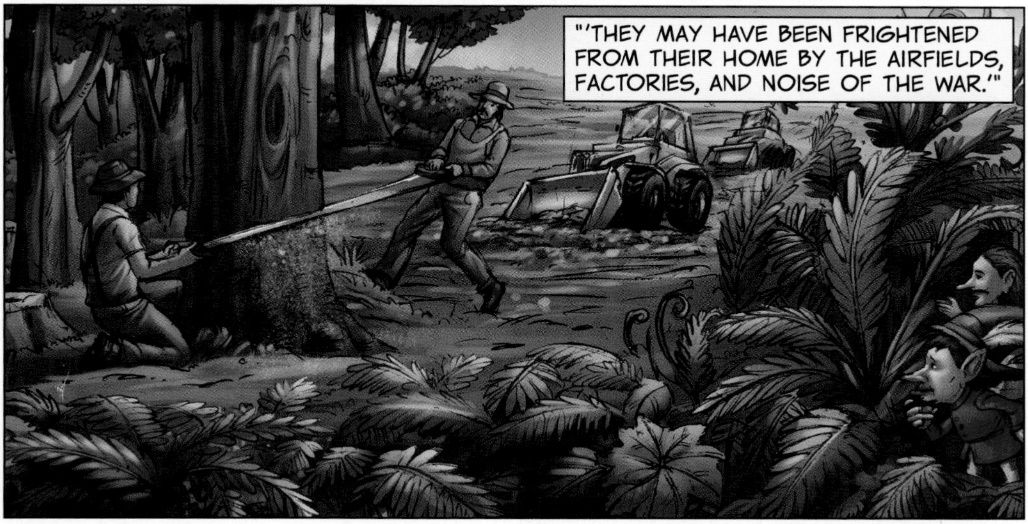
"'THEY MAY HAVE BEEN FRIGHTENED FROM THEIR HOME BY THE AIRFIELDS, FACTORIES, AND NOISE OF THE WAR.'"

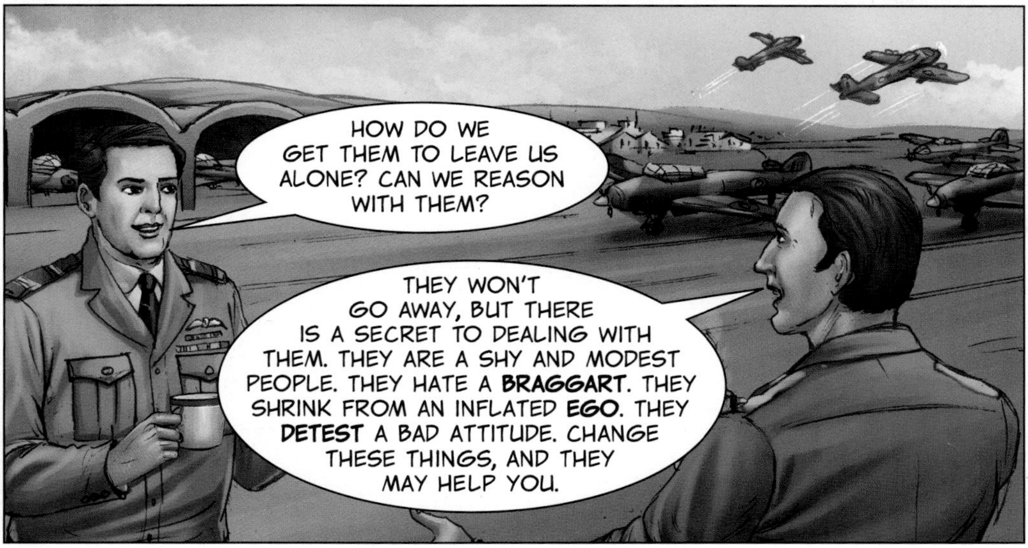
HOW DO WE GET THEM TO LEAVE US ALONE? CAN WE REASON WITH THEM?
THEY WON'T GO AWAY, BUT THERE IS A SECRET TO DEALING WITH THEM. THEY ARE A SHY AND MODEST PEOPLE. THEY HATE A **BRAGGART**. THEY SHRINK FROM AN INFLATED **EGO**. THEY **DETEST** A BAD ATTITUDE. CHANGE THESE THINGS, AND THEY MAY HELP YOU.

"SOME TIME LATER, GRIFFITH AND HIS CREW WENT ON A DANGEROUS MISSION."

WE HAVE BEEN HIT!

THE WINGS ARE PRETTY SHOT UP. WE ARE LOSING FUEL.

THE FUEL LEAKS HAVE STOPPED. HOW DID THAT HAPPEN?

LITTLE ANGELS ARE KEEPING US ALIVE.

"GRIFFITH LOOKED OUT THE WINDOW AND COULDN'T BELIEVE WHAT HE SAW."

"AS THE ATTITUDES OF THE FLIERS CHANGED, THE GREMLINS HELPED THEM. SOME THINK THIS CHANGED THE COURSE OF THE WAR."

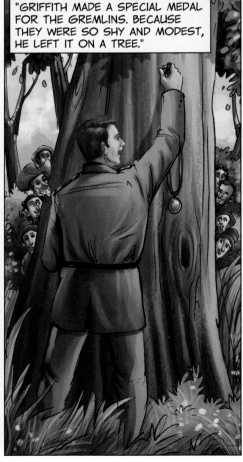

"GRIFFITH MADE A SPECIAL MEDAL FOR THE GREMLINS. BECAUSE THEY WERE SO SHY AND MODEST, HE LEFT IT ON A TREE."

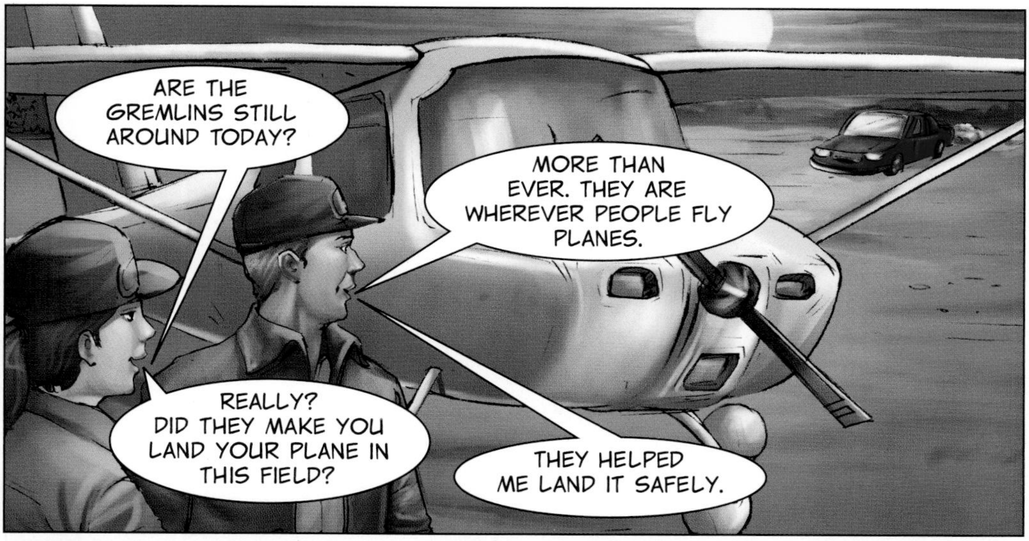
ARE THE GREMLINS STILL AROUND TODAY?
MORE THAN EVER. THEY ARE WHEREVER PEOPLE FLY PLANES.
REALLY? DID THEY MAKE YOU LAND YOUR PLANE IN THIS FIELD?
THEY HELPED ME LAND IT SAFELY.

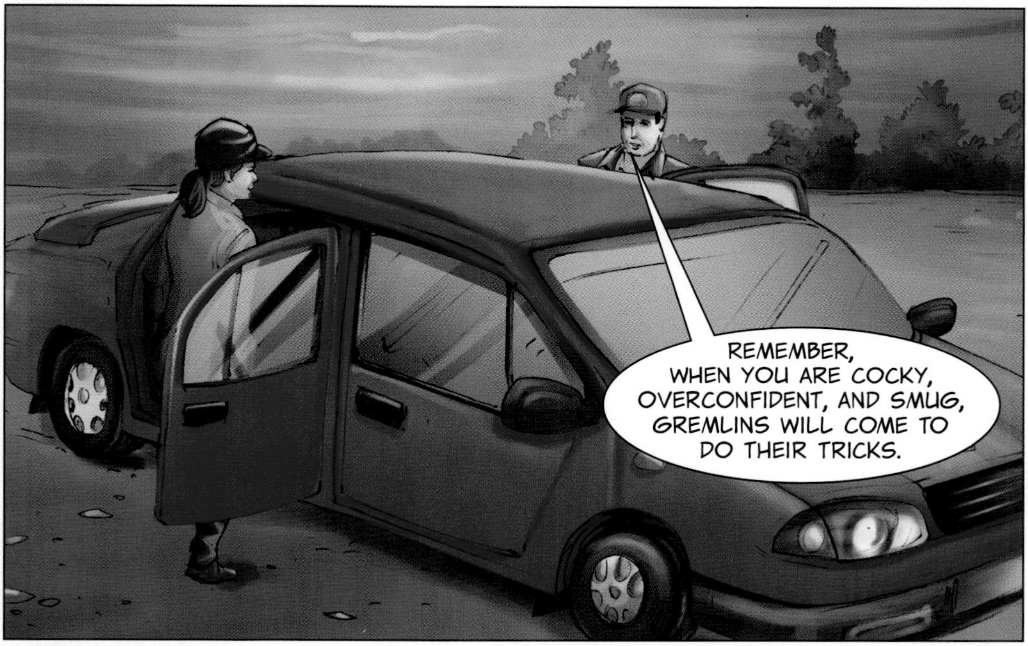
REMEMBER, WHEN YOU ARE COCKY, OVERCONFIDENT, AND SMUG, GREMLINS WILL COME TO DO THEIR TRICKS.

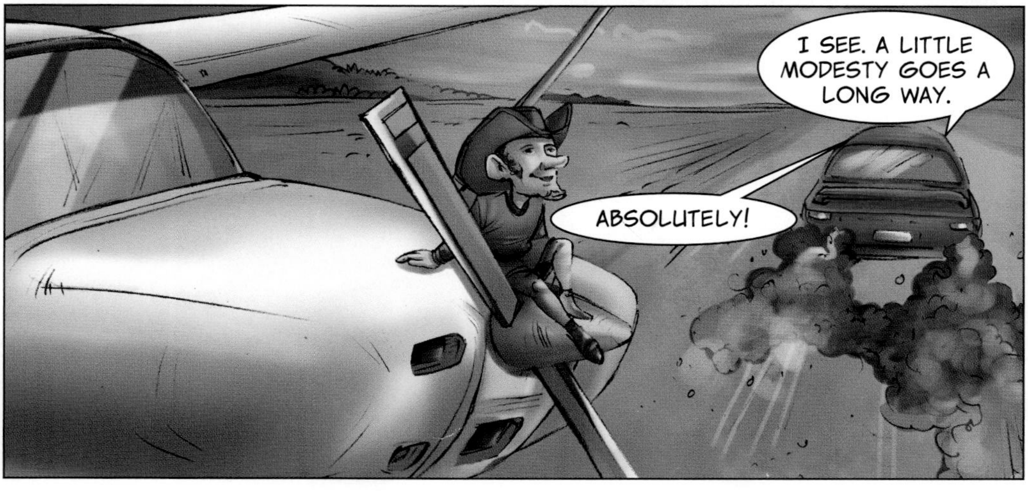
I SEE. A LITTLE MODESTY GOES A LONG WAY.
ABSOLUTELY!

More Little People Stories

- There are many Native American legends that involve little people. The little people of the **Cherokee** were about 1 to 2 feet (30–61 cm) tall. They belonged to various groups known as the Laurel People, the Rock People, and the Dogwood People. They lived in caves deep in the forest and were both happy and beautiful. They spent much of their time making music, singing, and dancing. Generally kindhearted, they often helped children lost in the woods. However, these little people loved their privacy and hated to be disturbed. If a stranger discovered their camp, they might cast a spell over him so he would walk around in a daze.

- **Choctaw** legend relates stories of people of the forest who were 2 or 3 feet (61–91 cm) tall. These little people would sometimes capture a young boy in the woods. They would take the boy far away, to their home, where they would teach him about special herbs, spells, and spirits so he would have the skills to treat the illnesses of the Choctaw people.

- **Dwarfs** and elves of **Scandinavian** legend lived deep in the forest, often in the mountains. They kept guard over a huge treasure of gold in deep underground caves. Some of them were highly skilled at working with metal. They made beautiful gifts for the **mythological** gods.

Glossary

aircraft carrier (AYR-kraft KAR-ee-ur) A ship with a deck on which planes can take off and land.

braggart (BRA-gurt) A person who boasts loudly about his or her accomplishments.

Cherokee (CHER-uh-kee) An American Indian group that originally lived in what is now Tennessee and North Carolina.

Choctaw (CHOK-taw) An American Indian group that originally lived in what is now Alabama, Mississippi, and Louisiana.

convoys (KON-voyz) Groups that travel together for safety.

detest (dih-TEST) To hate intensely.

devious (DEE-vee-us) Secretive and not straightforward.

dwarfs (DWARFS) Small people in stories who are ugly and misshapen and usually skilled craftsmen.

ego (EE-goh) A person's sense of his or her own importance.

escorted (is-KORT-ed) Went with someone to give him or her protection.

fighters (FY-terz) Planes used for fighting other planes in the air.

Gibraltar (juh-BRAHL-tur) A British territory on the Mediterranean coast of Spain.

Hawker Hurricane (HAH-ker HUR-ih-kayn) A British single-seat fighter aircraft.

leprechauns (LEP-ruh-konz) Elves from Irish fairy tales.

Mediterranean (meh-duh-teh-RAY-nee-un) Having to do with the area around the Mediterranean Sea.

mythological (mih-thuh-LAH-jih-kul) Made up, as stories.

Scandinavian (skan-duh-NAY-vee-un) Having to do with Scandinavia, the part of northern Europe that includes Norway, Sweden, and Denmark.

Index

Websites

Due to the changing nature of Internet links, PowerKids Press has developed an online list of websites related to the subject of this book. This site is updated regularly. Please use this link to access the list:

www.powerkidslinks.com/mons/grem